This gift is for:

_____

Who is deeply loved by:

_____

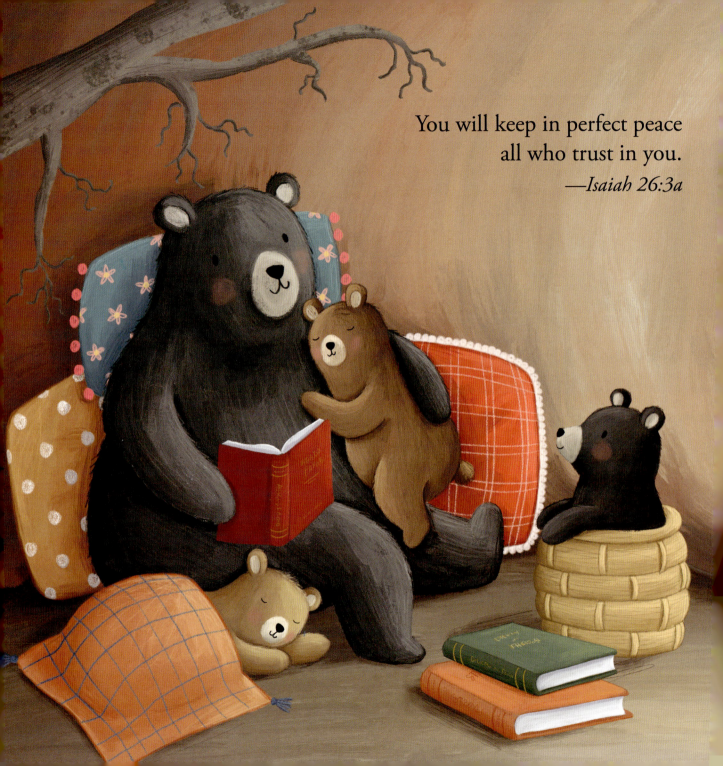

You will keep in perfect peace all who trust in you.
—Isaiah 26:3a

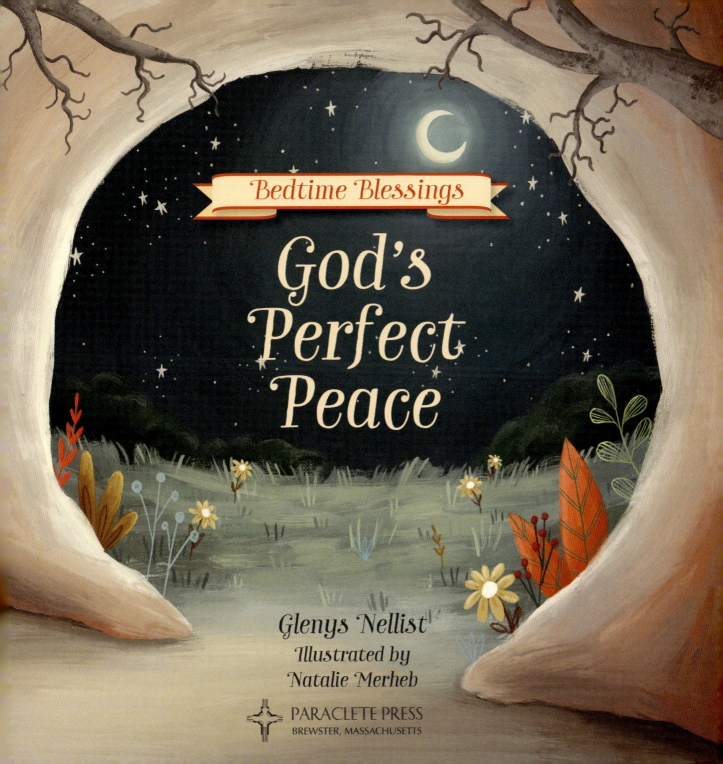

Little One, I pray for you,
As you lie down to sleep,

That you will know you're gently held
In our God's perfect peace.

God's peace is like a blanket,
That keeps you safe and snug.

God's peace is like a whisper
Or the gentlest, warmest hug.

May God's peace hover over you
On silent, whispery wings.

And may you know how much you're loved
As our God gently sings.

And if you wake up in the night,
You do not need to fear.

Remember, you are not alone...
The God of peace is here.

May God's peace give you stillness,
May God's peace keep you calm.

May God's peace fill this very room,
And keep you from all harm.

Little One, I pray for you,
As you drift off to sleep,

There is power in speaking blessings over your child. After you finish reading this book to your little one, gently trace the shape of a cross or a heart on their forehead (or palm) as you say a blessing over them. If your child is awake, look into their eyes. Fill in your child's name in the spaces below and use any of the following blessings:

_____, may God fill you with perfect peace. *(Isaiah 26:3)*

_____, in peace, may you lie down and sleep. *(Psalm 4:8)*

_____, may the God of hope fill you with joy and peace. *(Romans 15:13)*

_____, you are a blessing, and I love you.

Glenys Nellist is a bestselling author of many children's books, including five popular series: *Love Letters from God*, *Snuggle Time*, *'Twas*, *Good News*, and *Little Mole*. Three of her books have been finalists in the ECPA Book of the Year awards. A former teacher, Glenys has a passion for bringing the Bible to life for young children and speaks regularly in schools and churches. She and her husband, David, are the proud parents of four adult children and the happy grandparents of four little ones.

Natalie Merheb was born one snowy night in the far north of the United States. She spends her time illustrating nature, animals, and recreations of classics. Natalie now lives in Dubai, a city of perpetual heat and sun, with her husband and twin daughters.

2024 First Printing
God's Perfect Peace
ISBN 978-1-64060-939-6
Text copyright © 2025 by Glenys Nellist.
Illustrations copyright © 2025 by Paraclete Press.
Scripture quotation is taken from the *Holy Bible*, New Living Translation, copyright ©1996, 2004, 2015 by Tyndale House Foundation. Used by permission of Tyndale House Publishers, Carol Stream, Illinois 60188. All rights reserved.

The Paraclete Press name and logo (dove on cross) are trademarks of Paraclete Press.
Library of Congress Control Number: 2024908201
10 9 8 7 6 5 4 3 2 1

All rights reserved. No portion of this book may be reproduced, stored in an electronic retrieval system, or transmitted in any form or by any means—electronic, mechanical, photocopy, recording, or any other—except for brief quotations in printed reviews, without the prior permission of the publisher.

Published by Paraclete Press
Brewster, Massachusetts
www.paracletepress.com
Manufactured by: RR DONNELLEY
GUANGDONG PRINTING SOLUTIONS CO.,LTD.
Printed September 2024, in Dongguan, Guangdong, China
Batch #: 20240910GPSL